Green Gables Knits

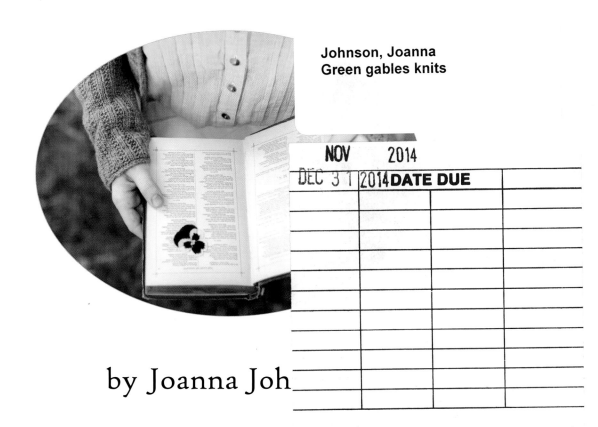

by Joanna Joh

Slate Falls Press
Loveland, Colorado

L. M. Montgomery is a trademark of Heirs of L. M. Montgomery, Inc.

Anne of Green Gables and other indicia of "Anne" are trademarks and Canadian Official Marks of the Anne of Green Gables Licensing Authority Inc.

"L. M. Montgomery" and "L. M. Montgomery's signature and cat design" are trademarks of Heirs of L. M. Montgomery, Inc.

All archival photographs printed with permission from the L. M. Montgomery Collection, Archival and Special Collections, University of Guelph Library

Slate Falls Press, LLC

P.O. Box 7062

Loveland, CO 80537

www.slatefallspress.com

Green Gables Knits/by Joanna Johnson

ISBN 978-0-578-12468-1 ISBN 0578124688

Signature Book Printing, Inc.

www.sbpbooks.com

Printed in the U.S.A.

dedicated to

my mom, J.D.B. and my sister, A.B.E.

for their encouragement, for being my sounding board, and

for helping me discover Anne in the first place

Lucy Maud Montgomery, age 14. L.M. Montgomery Collection,
Archival and Special Collections, University of Guelph Library.

The difficulty levels of the patterns in this book are marked by a number of carrots, with a single carrot indicating a simpler project, and up to three carrots indicating an increased challenge. Patterns with two or three carrots may include cables, lace charts, or working a variety of increases and decreases. Please note that even the more difficult patterns in the book are still perfectly suitable for an intermediate knitter. I hope you enjoy knitting these patterns as much as I enjoyed creating them! ~Joanna

Abbreviation Chart

beg beginning

BO bind off

CO cast on

dec decrease(d)

dpn double-pointed needle

inc increase(d)

k2tog knit two together

k3tog knit three together

k knit

kfb knit in front & back of stitch

kw knitwise

m marker

m1 make one by knitting into the back of the loop just below the next stitch

M1L insert left needle, from front to back, under the bar between the stitch just worked and the next stitch to create a loop, knit into the back of the loop

M1R insert left needle, from back to front, under the bar between the stitch just worked and the next stitch to create a loop, knit into the front of the loop

p purl

p2sso pass two slipped stitches over

p2tog purl 2 together

patt pattern

pfb purl in front & back of stitch

pm place marker

psso pass slipped stitch over

pw purlwise

rem remain

rnd round

RS right side

sl slip

sl m slip marker

ssk slip, slip, knit

st stitch

sts stitches

st st stockinette stitch

ws wrong side

wyib with yarn in back

wyif with yarn in front

yo yarn over

Kensington Train Station, P.E.I., ca. 1895. L.M. Montgomery Collection, Archival and Special Collections, University of Guelph Library.

"I've got all my worldly goods in it, but it isn't heavy. And if it isn't carried in just a certain way the handle pulls out ~ so I'd better keep it because I know the exact knack of it." ~Anne

Anne's Carpet Bag

Finished Measurements

Width at base after felting: 21 inches (53 cm)

Height from base to top after felting: 18 inches (46 cm)

Yarn

Brown Sheep Company Shepherd's Shades; 100% wool; 131 yards (118 meters) per 100 gram skein. Color A, Wild Asparagus, 3 skeins; Color B, Eggplant, 3 skeins; Color C, Marsh Grass, 2 skeins.

Needles

Size US 10½ (6.5 mm) circular needles, 32 inches (80 cm)

Change needle size if necessary to obtain the correct gauge.

Notions

Stitch markers, tapestry needle, stitch holder.

Homestead Heirlooms handle and magnet closure set, www.homesteadheirlooms.com :

1 pair of 20" sewn round solid leather core handles with loop and rivet ending

14" dowel and finial set, unassembled

Flower magnet with brown leather disk

Optional: 6½" x 20" (16.5 x 51 cm) thin masonite to support bag base

Gauge

12 sts and 16 rows = 4" (10 cm) in stockinette stitch before felting, 12 sts and 28 rows = 4" (10

This heavy worsted yarn felts beautifully; please take note of the gauge before and after felting, and you will see that it shrinks considerably in length, but not in width, after felting. Your bag will seem very tall before you felt it, but do not fear! It will look nicely proportioned after felting.

Notes

This project begins with the knitting of the rectangular base of the bag. Then, stitches are picked up around the base, and the bag is worked in the round upward. The bag is then divided and worked separately to create the top opening and handle casings. The pattern includes instructions for adding an optional interior pocket.

Difficulty Level:

Pattern

Bag Base:

With Color A, CO 71 sts.

Begin working back and forth, and work 42 rows in st st.

Bag Sides:

You will now begin working around the base of the bag and knitting in the round.

Knit 71 sts. Pick up and knit 20 sts along short side of base, 71 sts along CO edge, and 20 sts along last side of base. 182 sts.

Being careful not to twist sts, place marker and join for working in the round.

Begin 12 row mosaic stitch pattern as follows, carrying the yarn up the rounds as you go:

Row 1: With B, * k1, sl 1 wyif * repeat across round.

Row 2: With C, knit.

Row 3: With A, * sl 1 wyif, k1 * repeat across round.

Row 4: With B, knit.

Row 5: With C, * k1, sl 1 wyif * repeat across round.

Row 6: With A, knit.

Row 7: With B, * sl 1 wyif, k1 * repeat across round.

Row 8: With C, knit.

Row 9: With A, * k1, sl 1 wyif * repeat across round.

Row 10: With B, knit.

Row 11: With C, * sl 1 wyif, k1 * repeat across round.

Row 12: With A, knit.

Repeat these 12 rounds a total of 7 times.

Leaving a tail for weaving in later, cut color A yarn.

With B, * k28, k2tog * 6 times, k2. 176 sts rem.

With B, k 3 rnds.

Begin 16 rounds of the embroidery check pattern as follows:

Row 1: With C, * sl 3 wyib, k5 * repeat across round.

Row 2: With C, * sl 3 wyib, p2, k1, p2 * repeat across round.

Row 3: With B, K5, * sl 1 wyib , k7, * repeat across round to last 3 sts, sl 1 wyib, k2.

6

Row 4: With B, k5, * sl 1 wyib , k7, * repeat across round to last 3 sts, sl 1 wyib, k2.

Row 5: With C, * sl 3 wyib, k5 * repeat across round.

Row 6: With C, * sl 3 wyib, p2, k1, p2 * repeat across round.

Row 7: With B, k5, * sl 1 wyib , k7, * repeat across round to last 3 sts, sl 1 wyib, k2.

Row 8: With B, knit across round.

Row 9: With C, k4, * sl 3 wyib, k5 * repeat across round to last 4 stitches, sl 3 wyib, k1.

Row 10: With C, p1, k1, p2, * sl 3 wyib, p2, k1, p2 * repeat across round to last 4 stitches, sl 3 wyib, p1.

Row 11: With B, k1, * sl 1 wyib, k7 * repeat across round to last 7 sts, sl 1 wyib, k6.

Row 12: With B, k1, * sl 1 wyib, k7 * repeat across round to last 7 sts, sl 1 wyib, k6.

Row 13: With C, k4, * sl 3 wyib, k5 * repeat across round to last stitch, sl 3 wyib, k1.

Row 14: With C, p1, k1, p2, * sl 3 wyib, p2, k1, p2 * repeat across round to last 4 stitches, sl 3 wyib, p1.

Row 15: With B, k1, * sl 1 wyib, k7 * repeat across round to last 7 sts, sl 1 wyib, k6.

Row 16: With B, knit across round.

Leaving a 12" (30 cm) tail, break color C yarn.

Bag Top:

Continuing in Color B, divide for top section.

You will now adjust beginning of round by 11 sts to center the opening at the top of the bag by working as follows:

Remove beginning of round marker. Knit 77, place side marker, k88, place side marker.

Knit 88 sts to side marker. Place remaining 88 sts on holder to be worked later.

Begin working back and forth, turn and purl 1 row.

Decrease row: K1 * k2tog, k1* repeat across row 29 times. 29 sts dec. 59 sts rem.

Purl 1 row.

Decrease row: K1 * k1, k2tog * 19 times, k1. 19 sts dec. 40 sts rem.

Work 19 rows in st st.

BO all sts.

Work other top section:

With RS facing, join Color B yarn and knit 1 row, purl 1 row.

Decrease row: K1 * k2tog, k1 * repeat across row 29 times. 29 sts dec. 59 sts rem.

Turn and purl 1 row.

Decrease row: K1 * k1, k2tog * 19 times, k1. 19 sts dec. 40 sts rem.

Work 19 rows in st st.

BO all sts.

(Optional) Pocket:

With B, CO 24 sts.

Working back and forth, work 36 rows in st st.

BO all sts.

Finishing:

Weave in ends.

Felt bag and pocket separately according to your preferred method.

After felting, create a casing for the handles by folding a 2-inch (5 cm) section of the top fabric over toward the inside of the bag. Securely seam the casing by stitching the cast off edge to the inside of the bag. Insert handle dowel through the casing, then slide the handles over the ends of the dowel, securing with the finials.

(Optional) Stitch pocket securely to the inside of the bag.

(Optional) For a sturdier bag, round the corners of the masonite and insert it into the base of the bag.

New Glasgow Road, P.E.I. L.M. Montgomery Collection, Archival and Special Collections, University of Guelph Library.

"He didn't mind how much I talked ~ he seemed to like it. I felt that he was a kindred spirit as soon as ever I saw him." ~ Anne

Matthew's Vest

Finished Measurements

Chest circumference: 32 (36, 40, 44, 50, 56) inches / 81 (91, 102, 112, 127, 142) cm

Yarn

Brown Sheep Company Lanaloft Worsted; 100% wool; 160 yards (146 meters) per 100 gram skein; color shown, Cliff Rock; 4 (4, 4, 6, 6, 7) skeins. Shown in size 40" (102 cm).

Needles

Size US 7 (4.5 mm) circular needles 16 inches (40 cm) and 24 inches (60 cm)

Size US 9 (5.5 mm) circular needles 24 inches (60 cm) or 32 inches (80 cm)

Change needle size if necessary to obtain the correct gauge.

Notions

Stitch markers, tapestry needle, stitch holders or scrap yarn, cable needle.

Gauge

15 sts and 22 rows = 4" (10 cm) in stockinette stitch, after blocking.

Borrow a sweater or vest from the intended recipient that fits him (or her) very nicely and measure the width of the garment around the chest. Use the measurements as a guide to select the correct size for a perfect fit. You can also lengthen or shorten the vest before you separate for the armhole openings to further perfect the fit.

Notes

The vest is worked in the round from the bottom up and is then divided at the armhole to be worked back and forth. The shoulders are joined with a three-needle bind-off before stitches are picked up around the armhole and neck openings to be worked in the round in garter ribbing.

Difficulty Level:

Stitch Guide:

Cable pattern worked in the round:

Round 1: Knit to marker, p2, slip 4 sts to cable needle and hold to front, knit 4, knit 4 from cable needle, p2, knit to end of round.

Rounds 2-6: Knit to first marker, p2, k3, p2, k3, p2, knit to end of round.

Round 7: Knit to marker, p2, slip 4 sts to cable needle and hold to front, knit 4, knit 4 from cable needle, p2, knit to end of round.

Rounds 8-18: Knit to first marker, p2, k3, p2, k3, p2, knit to end of round.

Cable pattern worked back and forth:

Row 1: Knit to marker, p2, slip 4 sts to cable needle and hold to front, knit 4, knit 4 from cable needle, p2, knit to end of round.

Even rows 2, 4, 6, 8, 10, 12, 14, 16, 18: Purl to m, k2, p3, k2, p3, k2, purl to end.

Rows 3 and 5: Knit to first marker, p2, k3, p2, k3, p2, knit to end of round.

Row 7: Knit to marker, p2, slip 4 sts to cable needle and hold to front, knit 4, knit 4 from cable needle, p2, knit to end of round.

Rows 9, 11, 13, 15, 17: Knit to first marker, p2, k3, p2, k3, p2, knit to end of round.

Pattern

Using longer size US 7 (4.5 mm) needle, CO 128 (144, 160, 176, 192, 208) sts. Being careful not to twist sts, place marker and join for working in the round. Begin working garter ribbing in the round as follows:

Round 1: * k2, p2 * repeat from * to * across rnd.

Round 2: Knit.

Repeat these two rounds until vest measures 2½ (2½, 3, 3, 4, 4) inches / 6.5 (6.5, 7.5, 7.5, 10, 10) cm from the cast on edge.

Set-up round: remove marker, k1, replace marker for new beginning of rnd. Then, k 26 (30, 34, 38, 42, 46), pm, k12 for cable panel, pm, k 26 (30, 34, 38, 42, 46), pm for side of vest, k 64 (72, 80, 88, 96, 104).

Switch to size US 9 (5.5 mm) needles and work set-up round as follows:

Set-up round: Knit to first marker, p2, k3, p2, k3, p2, knit to end of round.

Repeat this round 7 times more.

Work the 18-round cable pattern in the round (see Stitch Guide above) until the vest measures 15 (15, 16, 16, 17, 17) inches / 38 (38, 41, 41, 43, 43) cm from the cast on edge, ending on an even number of the pattern rows. Remember what number row you ended on.

You are now going to divide the front and back for the armhole opening.

Place 64 (72, 80, 88, 96, 104) sts for back of the vest on a holder or scrap yarn.

You will now begin working back and forth on the vest front, beginning with the RS facing you. Work the 18-row cable pattern back and forth (see Stitch Guide) starting with the next number row from where you left off and at the same time, BO 6 (6, 7, 7, 8, 8) sts, work across row in pattern. 58 (66, 73, 81, 88, 96) sts rem.

Next row: BO 6 (6, 7, 7, 8, 8) sts, purl to m, k2, p3, k2, p3, k2, purl to end. 52 (60, 66, 74, 80, 88) sts rem.

Keeping in this pattern as established, BO 2 (2, 3, 3, 4, 4) sts at beg of next two rows, 2 (2, 2, 3, 3, 3) sts at the beg of the next two rows, and 1 st at the beg of the next two rows. 42 (50, 54, 60, 64, 72) sts rem.

Divide for V-neck:

Knit to m, p2, k2, k2tog. Place remaining 21 (25, 27, 30, 32, 36) sts on a holder for the other side.

Turn and p3, k2, purl to end of row. 20 (24, 26, 29, 31, 35) sts rem.

Next row, work decrease row: knit to 2 sts before m, ssk, p2, k3. 19 (23, 25, 28, 30, 34) sts rem.

Next row, as established: P3, k2, purl to end.

Repeat these two rows twice more. 17 (21, 23, 26, 28, 32) sts rem.

Continue shaping neck:

Row 1: Work decrease row: knit to 2 sts before m, ssk, p2, k3.

Row 2: P3, k2, purl to end.

Row 3: Knit to m, p2, k3.

Row 4: P3, k2, purl to end.

Repeat these four rows 4 (5, 6, 7, 8, 9) times more. 12 (15, 16, 18, 19, 22) sts rem.

Then, repeat rows 3 and 4 twice more.

Break yarn, place sts on a holder to be joined to the back shoulder strap later.

Work other half of front using sts from holder:

Beginning with RS facing, k2tog, k2, p2, knit to end. 20 (24, 26, 29, 31, 35) sts rem.

Purl to m, k2, p3.

Next row, work decrease row: k3, p2, k2tog, knit to end. 19 (23, 25, 29, 31, 35) sts rem.

Next row, as established: purl to m, k2, p3.

Repeat these two rows twice more. 17 (21, 23, 26, 28, 32) sts rem.

Continue shaping neck:

Row 1: Work decrease row: k3, p2, k2tog, knit to end.

Row 2: Purl to m, k2, p3.

Row 3: K3, p2, knit to end.

Row 4: Purl to m, k2, p3.

Repeat these four rows 4 (5, 6, 7, 8, 9) times more. 12 (15, 16, 18, 19, 22) sts.

Then, repeat rows 3 and 4 twice more.

Break yarn, place sts on a holder to be joined to the back shoulder strap later.

Work back of vest using sts from holder:

Begin working with RS facing, working in st st. (Knit on RS row, purl on WS row).

BO 6 (6, 7, 7, 8, 8) sts, knit to end.

Next row: BO 6 (6, 7, 7, 8, 8) sts, purl to end.

Keeping as established in stockinette stitch, BO 2 (2, 3, 3, 4, 4) sts at beg of next two rows, 2 (2, 2, 3, 3, 3) sts at beg of next two rows, 1 st at beg of next two rows. 42 (50, 54, 60, 64, 72) sts rem.

Work 27 (31, 35, 39, 41, 43) rows in st st, ending on a RS row.

BO for neck (WS row): p 14 (17, 18, 20, 21, 24) sts and place sts on a holder; BO 14 (16, 18, 20, 22, 24) sts for back of neck; p 14 (17, 18, 20, 21, 24) sts.

Shape back neck: knit to last 2 sts, k2tog.

Purl across row.

Knit to last 2 sts, k2tog.

Purl across row.

Break yarn, place 12 (15, 16, 18, 19, 22) sts on holder to be joined to the front shoulder strap later.

Work other side, beginning with RS facing: ssk, knit to end of row.

Purl across row.

Ssk, knit to end of row.

Purl across row.

Break yarn, place 12 (15, 16, 18, 19, 22) sts on holder to be joined to the front shoulder strap.

Using three-needle bind-off, join left front to left back shoulder. Repeat for the right shoulder.

Armhole edging:

Using the shorter size US 7 (4.5 mm) needle and beginning at the bottom of the armhole opening, pick up and knit 80 (88, 96, 104, 112, 124) sts around armhole opening. Being careful not to twist stitches, place marker and join for working in the round.

Round 1: * p2, k2 * repeat from * across round.

Round 2: Knit.

Repeat these two rounds once more.

BO all sts kw.

Repeat for the other armhole opening.

Neck edging:

Using the shorter size US 7 (4.5 mm) needle and beginning at the shoulder opening, pick up and knit 76 (84, 92, 100, 112, 120) sts around neck opening. Being careful not to twist stitches, place marker and join for working in the round.

Round 1: * p2, k2 * repeat from * across round.

Round 2: Knit.

Repeat these two rounds once more.

BO all sts kw.

Finishing:

Weave in ends and block.

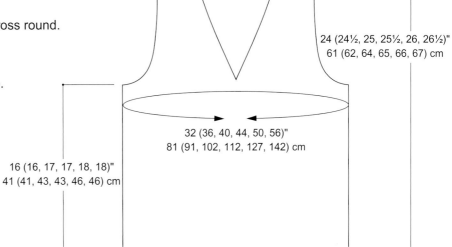

24 (24½, 25, 25½, 26, 26½)"
61 (62, 64, 65, 66, 67) cm

32 (36, 40, 44, 50, 56)"
81 (91, 102, 112, 127, 142) cm

16 (16, 17, 17, 18, 18)"
41 (41, 43, 43, 46, 46) cm

Old Cavendish kitchen, ca. 1895. Cavendish, P.E.I. L.M. Montgomery Collection, Archival and Special Collections, University of Guelph Library.

"Miss Marilla Cuthbert is a very kind lady who has taken me to bring up properly. She is doing her best, but it is very discouraging work." ~Anne

Marilla's Apron

Finished Measurements

Width at waist: 16" (41 cm)

Width at hem: 24" (61 cm)

Width of sash: 90" (229 cm)

Yarn

Brown Sheep Company Cotton Fleece; 80% cotton, 20% wool; 215 yards (197 meters) per 100 gram skein; color shown, Honey Butter; 3 skeins.

Needles

Size US 6 (4.0 mm) circular needles, 24 inches (60 cm).

Crochet hook size F (3.75 mm)

Change needle size if necessary to obtain the correct gauge.

Gauge

20 sts and 26 rows = 4" (10 cm) in stockinette stitch, after blocking.

To lengthen this apron into a more formal accessory, simply work the lace repeat a total of five times rather than three times. Be sure to buy an extra skein of yarn to accommodate accordingly.

Notes

Knit from the hem up, this stylish apron features the "Old Fern" lace stitch and a long sash that ties in the back. Single crochet is worked around the entire edge of the apron for a tidy finish.

Difficulty Level:

Pattern

CO 109 sts.

Begin working 20-row "Old Fern" lace pattern 3 times total, either according to the chart or to the written instructions:

Rows 1, 3, 5: K2tog, * k2, yo, ssk, yo, k1, yo, k2tog, yo, k2, k3tog * repeat from * to * ending last repeat with ssk.

All even rows: purl.

Row 7: K2tog, * k1, yo, k2tog, yo, k3, yo, ssk, yo, k1, k3tog * repeat from * to * ending last repeat with ssk.

Row 9: K2tog, * yo, k2tog, yo, k5, yo, ssk, yo, k3tog * repeat from * to * ending last repeat with ssk.

Rows 11, 13, 15: K1, * yo, k2tog, yo, k2, k3tog, k2, yo, ssk, yo, k1 * repeat from * to *.

Row 17: K1 * k1, yo, ssk, yo, k1, k3tog, k1, yo, k2tog, yo, k2 * repeat from * to *.

Row 19: K1 * k2, yo, ssk, yo, k3tog, yo, k2tog, yo, k3 * repeat from * to *.

You have now completed 60 rows, having worked the 20-row lace pattern three times. Continue as follows:

Next row: K4 * ssk, yo, k1, yo, k2tog, k7 * repeat from * to *, ending last repeat with k4 instead of k7.

Next row: Purl.

Repeat these two rows twice more.

Next row: K6 * sl1 wyib, k11 * repeat from * to *, ending last repeat with k6 instead of k11.

Next row: Purl.

Repeat these two rows 4 times more.

Decrease row: K4 * ssk, sl1 wyib, k2tog, k7 * repeat from * to *, ending last repeat with k4 instead of k7. 18 sts dec. 91 sts rem.

Next row: Purl.

Continue as follows:

Next row: K5 * sl1 wyib, k9 * repeat from * to *, ending last repeat with k5 instead of k9.

Next row: Purl.

Repeat these two rows 9 times more.

Decrease row: K3, * ssk, sl1 wyib, k2tog, k5 * repeat from * to *, ending last repeat with k3 instead of k5. 18 sts dec. 73 sts rem.

Next row: Purl.

Continue as follows:

Next row: K4, * sl1 wyib, k7 * repeat from * to *, ending last repeat with k4 instead of k7.

Next row: Purl.

Repeat these two rows 7 times more.

Cast on for sash:

Knit across row, do not turn. CO 152 sts using backward loop cast on. 225 sts.

Next row: knit across row, do not turn, CO 151 sts using backward loop cast on. 376 sts.

Begin pattern for sash:

Row 1: Knit.

Row 2: * K1, sl 1 wyib * repeat from * to * to last 2 sts, k2.

Row 3: Knit.

Row 4: K2, * sl1 wyib, k1 * repeat from * to *.

Work this four-row pattern twice more.

Knit 2 rows.

BO all sts.

Edging:

Using crochet hook, and beginning at lower right corner of hem, work single crochet (sc) across the hem and around the entire edge of the apron, including the sash. Work in a ratio of 1 sc per knit stitch across the hem, 2 sc per 3 rows along side of apron, 1 sc per stitch around the sash, and 2 sc per 3 rows along the other side of the apron.

Finishing:

Weave in ends and block.

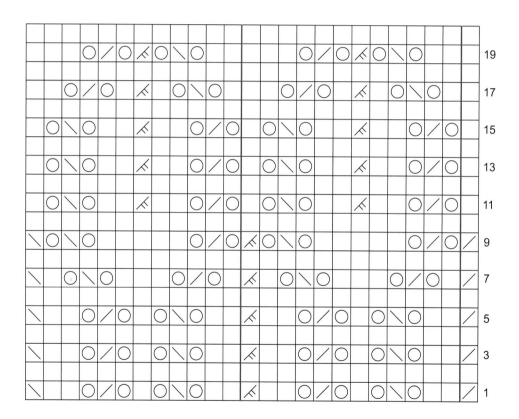

Pond at Park Corner, ca. 1890's, known as Lake of Shining Waters in Anne of Green Gables.
L.M. Montgomery Collection, Archival and Special Collections, University of Guelph Library.

The way Anne and Diana went to school was a pretty one. Anne thought those walks to and from school with Diana couldn't be improved upon even by imagination.

Diana's Hat

Finished Measurements

Hat circumference at lower edge:
26" (66 cm), stretched.

Yarn

Brown Sheep Company Lamb's Pride Superwash Sport; 100% wool; 180 yards (165 meters) per 50 gram skein; color shown, Frosted Fuchsia; 1 skein. Sample knitters used nearly an entire skein of yarn to create this hat; circumspect knitters may wish to purchase an additional skein of yarn for this project.

Needles

Size US 4 (3.5 mm) circular needles, 16 inches (40 cm).

Size US 4 (3.5 mm) dpns.

Change needle size if necessary to obtain the correct gauge.

Notions

Stitch markers, tapestry needle, a dinner plate for blocking.

Gauge

24 sts = 4" (10 cm) in stockinette stitch, after blocking.

To create a lovely "slouchy" drape on this hat, block by soaking for 20-30 minutes in a no-rinse solution for hand knits. By blocking the hat over an upside-down plate as described in the instructions, you will obtain the perfect shape for this simple but flattering hat.

Notes

This simple and stylish hat is worked in the round from the edge up. A quick knit, it would make a lovely gift for your bosom friends.

Difficulty Level:

Pattern

Using circular needles, CO 100 sts.

Being careful not to twist sts, pm and join for working in the round.

Round 1: purl.

Round 2: knit.

Round 3: purl.

Round 4: knit.

Round 5: purl.

Increase round: kfb every st. 100 sts inc. 200 sts rem.

Knit five rounds.

Decrease round: k2tog across round. 100 sts dec. 100 sts rem.

Round 1: purl.

Round 2: knit.

Round 3: purl.

Round 4: knit.

Round 5: purl.

Increase round: kfb every st. 100 sts inc. 200 sts rem.

Knit five rounds.

Decrease round: k2tog across round. 100 sts dec. 100 sts rem.

Round 1: purl.

Round 2: knit.

Round 3: purl.

Round 4: knit.

Round 5: purl.

Increase round: * k1, kfb * repeat from * to * across rnd. 50 sts inc. 150 sts rem.

Knit every round for 22 rounds.

Shape top of hat:

(K13, k2tog) 10 times. 10 sts dec. 140 sts rem. Knit 1 round.

(K12, k2tog) 10 times. 10 sts dec. 130 sts rem. Knit 1 round.

(K11, k2tog) 10 times, 10 sts dec. 120 sts rem. Knit 1 round.

(K10, k2tog) 10 times. 10 sts dec. 110 sts rem. Knit 1 round.

Continue decreasing in this manner, working one knit round between each decrease round, until 10 sts remain.

K2tog 5 times.

Break yarn, leaving a tail, draw yarn through five remaining sts, and fasten.

Finishing:

Weave in ends. Block by soaking hat for 20-30 minutes in a no-rinse solution for handknits. Gently stretch hat around a dinner plate, centering the top of the hat on the bottom of the plate, and gathering the hem around the edge of the top of the plate. Place the plate upside-down and allow the hat to air dry.

Dining Room of Leaksdale Manse. L.M. Montgomery Collection, Archival and Special Collections, University of Guelph Library.

...Mrs. Rachel Lynde was one of those capable creatures who can manage their own concerns and those of other folks into the bargain.

Rachel's Table Runner

Finished Measurements

Width: 12" (31 cm)

Length: 30" (76 cm)

Yarn

Brown Sheep Company Cotton Fine; 80% cotton, 20% wool; 215 yards (202 meters) per 50 gram skein; color shown, Cotton Ball; 2 skeins.

Needles

Size US 3 (3.25 mm) circular or straight needles

Change needle size if necessary to obtain the correct gauge.

Notions

Stitch markers, tapestry needle, blocking wires as needed.

Gauge

26 sts and 30 rows = 4" (10 cm) in stockinette stitch, after blocking.

It would be simple to adjust this pattern to make placemats instead of a tablerunner. Follow directions as written, except work the table runner in a shorter length to make the placemats. You will use a little less than one skein per placemat.

Notes

The edging for this table runner is worked as you go, making this a seamless accessory for your home. You can customize the length by working it shorter or longer than shown, according to your preference.

Difficulty Level:

Pattern

Cast on 79 sts.

Begin working Chart A:

Row 1: K1, * k1, k2tog, yo, k1, yo, ssk, k1 * repeat from * to last st, k1.

Row 2: Purl.

Row 3: K1 * k2tog, yo, k3, yo, ssk * repeat from * to last st, k1.

Row 4: Purl.

Repeat these four rows three times more.

Work rows 1-3 once more.

Next row: place markers for next section: purl 15, pm, purl 49, pm, purl 15.

Begin working Chart B:

Row 1: K1, * k1, k2tog, yo, k1, yo, ssk, k1 * repeat from * once more, sl m, k 49 to next marker, * k1, k2tog, yo, k1, yo, ssk, k1 * repeat from * once more, k1.

Row 2: Purl.

Row 3: K1, * k2tog, yo, k3, yo, ssk * repeat from * once more, sl m, k 49 to next marker, * k2tog, yo, k3, yo, ssk * repeat from * once more, k1.

Row 4: Purl

Work in pattern for Chart B until the table runner measures 28" (71 cm) from CO edge.

Work Chart A:

Row 1: K1, * k1, k2tog, yo, k1, yo, ssk, k1 * repeat from * to last st, k1.

Row 2: Purl.

Row 3: K1 * k2tog, yo, k3, yo, ssk * repeat from * to last st, k1.

Row 4: Purl.

Work these four rows four times more.

Bind off all sts.

Finishing:

Weave in ends. Block, using wires as necessary to keep the edges straight.

Chart A

3

1

	K on RS, P on WS
\	ssk
/	K2tog
O	YO

Chart B

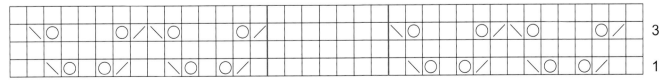

3

1

Group of children outside Cavendish school house, ca. 1880's. Cavendish, P.E.I. L.M. Montgomery Collection, Archival and Special Collections, University of Guelph Library.

"I love Miss Stacy with my whole heart, Marilla. She is so lady~like and has such a sweet voice. When she pronounces my name I feel instinctively that she is spelling it with an e." ~Anne

Miss Stacy's Shawl

Finished Measurements

Length across neckline: 28" (71 cm)

Length across hem: 82" (208 cm)

Yarn

Brown Sheep Company Nature Spun Fingering; 100% wool; 310 yards (283 meters) per 50 gram skein; color shown, Butterscotch; 3 skeins.

Needles

Size US 5 (3.75 mm) circular needles, 24 inches (60 cm) or longer

Change needle size if necessary to obtain the correct gauge.

Notions

Stitch markers, tapestry needle, blocking pins and wires as needed.

Optional: shawl pin.

Gauge

24 sts and 36 rows = 4" (10 cm) in stockinette stitch, after blocking.

*When working a lace pattern over a large number of stitches, as you do on this shawl, it helps to use stitch markers to separate the pattern repeats. Simply place a stitch marker between each lace pattern repeat, as indicated in the instructions with a " * ". This way it is easier to identify an error should your stitch count be off.*

Notes

This stitch pattern is a variation of the classic "Feather and Fan" lace stitch. Rows 3, 7, 11, and 15 are the same. Then the pattern shifts and rows 19, 23, 27, and 31 are the same. The remainder of the pattern rows are worked in stockinette stitch.

Difficulty Level:

Pattern

Cast on 481 sts.

Work lace pattern over 32 rows as follows:

Row 1: knit.

Row 2: purl.

Row 3: (K1, yo) three times, * (ssk) twice; sl 2 kw at the same time, k1, p2sso; (k2tog) twice; (yo, k1) five times; yo * repeat from * to * to last 14 sts, then, (ssk) twice; sl 2 kw at the same time, k1, p2sso; (k2tog) twice; (yo, k1) three times.

Row 4: purl.

Row 5: knit.

Row 6: purl.

Row 7: (K1, yo) three times, * (ssk) twice; sl 2 kw at the same time, k1, p2sso; (k2tog) twice; (yo, k1) five times; yo * repeat from * to * to last 14 sts, then, (ssk) twice; sl 2 kw at the same time, k1, p2sso; (k2tog) twice; (yo, k1) three times.

Row 8: purl.

Row 9: knit.

Row 10: purl.

Row 11: (K1, yo) three times, * (ssk) twice; sl 2 kw at the same time, k1, p2sso; (k2tog) twice; (yo, k1) five times; yo * repeat from * to * to last 14 sts, then, (ssk) twice; sl 2 kw at the same time, k1, p2sso; (k2tog) twice; (yo, k1) three times.

Row 12: purl.

Row 13: knit.

Row 14: purl.

Row 15: (K1, yo) three times, * (ssk) twice; sl 2 kw at the same time, k1, p2sso; (k2tog) twice; (yo, k1) five times; yo * repeat from * to * to last 14 sts, then, (ssk) twice; sl 2 kw at the same time, k1, p2sso; (k2tog) twice; (yo, k1) three times.

Row 16: purl.

Row 17: knit.

Row 18: purl.

Row 19: (K2tog) three times, * (yo, k1) five times; yo; (ssk) twice; sl 2 kw at the same time, k1, p2sso; (k2tog) twice * repeat from * to * to last 11 sts, then, (yo, k1) five times; yo; (ssk) three times.

Row 20: purl.

Row 21: knit.

Row 22: purl.

Row 23: (K2tog) three times, * (yo, k1) five times; yo; (ssk) twice; sl 2 kw at the same time, k1, p2sso; (k2tog) twice * repeat from * to * to last 11 sts, then, (yo, k1) five times; yo; (ssk) three times.

Row 24: purl.

Row 25: knit.

Row 26: purl.

Row 27: (K2tog) three times, * (yo, k1) five times; yo; (ssk) twice; sl 2 kw at the same time, k1, p2sso; (k2tog) twice * repeat from * to * to last 11 sts, then, (yo, k1) five times; yo; (ssk) three times.

Row 28: purl.

Row 29: knit.

Row 30: purl.

Row 31: (K2tog) three times, * (yo, k1) five times; yo; (ssk) twice; sl 2 kw at the same time, k1, p2sso; (k2tog) twice * repeat from * to * to last 11 sts, then, (yo, k1) five times; yo; (ssk) three times.

Row 32: purl.

Work 32-row pattern once more.

Decrease row: K2tog across row 239 times to last 3 sts, then, k3tog once, 241 sts dec. 240 sts rem.

Begin working in stockinette stitch with garter edging:

Row 1: K3, purl to last 3 sts, k3.

Row 2: Knit.

Work in stockinette stitch with garter edging for a total of 47 rows.

Decrease row: K1, * k2tog, k2 * repeat from * to * 59 times to last 3 sts, k2tog, k1. 60 sts dec. 180 sts rem.

Work in stockinette stitch with garter edging for 23 rows.

Decrease row: K1, * k2tog, k2 * repeat from * to * 44 times to last 3 sts, k2tog, k1. 45 sts dec. 135 sts rem.

Knit 4 rows.

Bind off all stitches.

Finishing:

Weave in ends.

Block, using pins and/or heat if desired to accentuate the lace pattern.

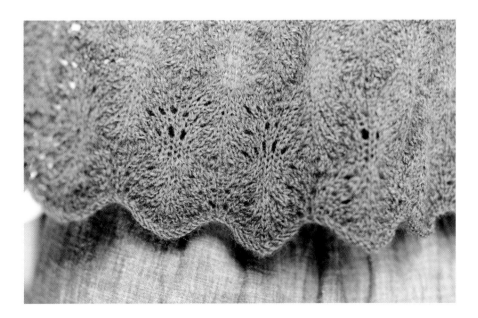

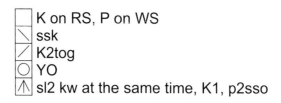

K on RS, P on WS
ssk
K2tog
YO
sl2 kw at the same time, K1, p2sso

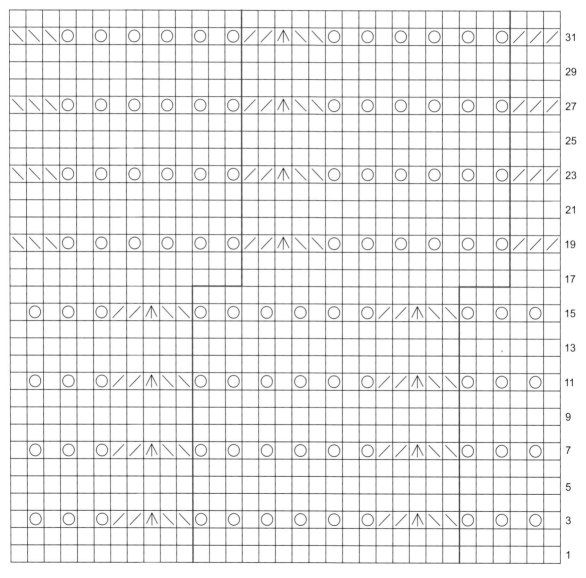

34

Orchard at Park Corner, P.E.I. L.M. Montgomery Collection, Archival and Special Collections, University of Guelph Library.

"…at heart I shall always be your little Anne, who will love you and Matthew and dear Green Gables more and better every day of her life." ~Anne

Anne's Sweater

Finished Measurements

Chest circumference: 30 (34, 38, 42, 46, 50, 54) inches / 76 (86, 97, 107, 117, 127, 137) cm. Select the size closest to your measurements, rounding down for a slimmer fit, and rounding up for a looser fit.

Yarn

Brown Sheep Company Lanaloft Sport; 100% wool; 145 yards (133 meters) per 50 gram skein; color shown, Scottish Hillside; 8 (9, 11, 13, 15, 16, 17) skeins. Shown in size 34" (86 cm).

Needles

Size US 5 (3.75 mm) 32 inch (80 cm) and 60 inch (150 cm) circular needles, size US 5 (3.75 mm) dpns.

Size US 7 (4.5 mm) 32 inch (80 cm) circular needles and dpns.

Change needle size if necessary to obtain the correct gauge.

Notions

Stitch markers, tapestry needle.

Gauge

20 sts and rows 26 rows= 4" (10 cm) in stockinette stitch on larger needle.

As this sweater is knit from the top down, you can easily customize the fit in a few key areas. Consider working more or less rows on the collar and pocket band, to increase or decrease the coverage across the bustline as you prefer. Also, as the sleeves are also worked top down, feel free to add or remove length to the sleeves according to your preference.

Notes

This cozy cardigan is knit from the top down and is nearly seamless. The pockets are worked as a part of the garter rib collar, and are folded up and seamed along the edge. The two smallest sizes, including the sweater shown above, are worked straight without shaping from the neck downward along the collar line. For all other sizes, increases are worked along the front edge to add more shaping to the bustline.

Difficulty Level:

Pattern

Using larger circular needle, CO 68 (82, 104, 120, 128, 140, 156) sts.

Work set up row: purl 2, pm, purl 16 (18, 26, 32, 34, 38, 44), pm, purl 32 (42, 48, 52, 56, 60, 64), pm, purl 16 (18, 26, 32, 34, 38, 44), pm, purl 2.

Begin raglan increases:

Row 1: * Knit to 1 st before m, M1R, k1, sl m, k1, M1L * repeat from * to * three times more. Knit to end.

Row 2: Purl.

8 sts inc over two rows.

Work these two rows a total of 10 (10, 9, 10, 14, 14, 12) times. 80 (80, 72, 80, 112, 112, 96) sts inc. 148 (162, 176, 200, 240, 252, 252) sts.

Continue increasing:

For sizes 30 (34, 38, 42) inches / 81 (86, 97, 107) cm only:

Row 1: * Knit to 1 st before m, M1R, k1, sl m, k1, M1L * repeat from * to * three times more. Knit to end.

Row 2: Purl.

Row 3: Knit.

Row 4: Purl.

8 sts inc over four rows.

Work these four rows a total of 9 (9, 7, 4) times. 72 (72, 56, 32) sts inc. 220 (234, 232, 232) sts.

For sizes 38 (42, 46, 50, 54) inches / 107 (117, 127, 137) cm only:

Row 1: * Knit to 1 st before m, M1R, k1, sl m, k1, M1L * repeat from * to * three times more. Knit to end.

Row 2: Purl.

Row 3: K3, M1L, knit to last 3 sts, M1R, knit 3.

Row 4: Purl.

10 sts inc over four rows.

Work these four rows a total of 3 (7, 10, 12, 16) times. 30 (70, 100, 120, 160) sts inc. 262 (302, 340, 372, 412) sts.

Separate for sleeves:

Knit to first marker, remove marker, place 54 (56, 64, 74, 82, 90, 100) sleeve sts on a holder to be worked later, leave marker as side marker, knit across 70 (80, 86, 94, 104, 112, 120) back sts to next marker, remove marker, place 54 (56, 64, 74, 82, 90, 100) sleeve sts on a holder to be worked later, leave marker as side marker, knit to end of row. 112 (122, 134, 154, 176, 192, 210) sts for body of sweater.

Body:

Work 9 rows even in st st, ending on a WS row.

Work decrease row: Knit to 2 sts past 1st side m, ssk, knit to 4 sts before next side marker, k2tog, knit to end of row. 2 sts dec.

Work next 7 rows in st st.

Repeat these 8 rows 5 times more. 100 (110, 122, 142, 164, 180, 198) sts.

Work increase row: Knit to 2 sts past the 1st side marker, M1L, knit to 2 sts before the next side marker, M1R, knit to end of row. 2 sts inc.

Work five rows in st st.

Work these 6 rows 7 times more. 116 (126, 138, 158, 180, 196, 214) sts.

Work hem:

Knit one row (RS).

Switch to size US 5 (3.75 mm) shorter circular needles and work in garter rib:

Row 1 (WS): * k2, p2 * repeat from * to * across row, ending k2 for sizes 34, 38, 42, and 54. (86, 97, 107, 137 cm).

Row 2 (RS): Knit.

Work 3 (3, 3½, 3½, 4, 4, 4) inches / 7.5 (7.5, 9, 9, 10, 10, 10) cm in garter rib, ending on a RS row.

BO all sts kw.

Collar and pockets:

You will now cast on for the pockets and pick up stitches for the collar. It works best when you pick up sts at a rate of 3 sts per four rows when working up the sweater fronts, and 1 st per st when picking up along the top of the sleeves and back of neck.

Switch to smaller size US 5 (3.75 mm) and longer circular needles. CO 30 sts to a spare size US 5 (3.75 mm) dpn for the right pocket. Continuing with this working yarn, using the longest size US 5 (3.75 mm) circular needle and working with RS of sweater facing, pick up and knit 119 (120, 128, 136, 144, 148, 153) sts along right side of sweater, 13 (15, 24, 30, 32, 36, 41) sts from sleeve section of sweater, 30 (40, 46, 50, 54, 58, 62) sts from back of sweater, 13 (15, 24, 30, 32, 36, 41) sts from sleeve section of sweater, 119 (120, 128, 136, 144, 148, 153) sts along left side of sweater, CO 30 sts to a spare size US 5 (3.75 mm) dpn for left pocket. 354 (370, 410, 442, 466, 486, 510) sts.

Work set up row, on WS: knit 30, pm, p2 * k2, p2 * to last 30 sts, pm, knit 30.

Work in pattern as follows:

Row 1 (RS row): p2 * k2, p2 * to m, knit to next m, p2 * k2, p2 * to end.

Row 2 (WS row): Knit to m, p2 * k2, p2 * to next m, knit to end.

Work these 2 rows for 3½ (4, 4½, 4½, 5, 5, 5) inches / 9 (10, 11, 11, 13, 13) cm, ending on a WS row.

Create pockets:

RS row: break yarn, leaving a tail for weaving in. Place last 30 sts of row to a holder to be worked later. Place first 30 sts of row on a spare dpn needle, remove marker, fold pocket toward RS of sweater. Attach new yarn. K2tog (one from each needle held together) 30 times to attach pocket to edge of cardigan. Knit across row to last 30 sts of row. Place 30 sts from holder on a spare dpn needle. Fold pocket toward RS of sweater. K2tog (one from each needle held together) 30 times to attach pocket to edge of cardigan.

Knit 1 row.

BO all sts kw.

Sleeves:

Place sts from holder for sleeve onto larger dpns. Place marker for beginning of the round and begin working.

Work in st st (knit every round) for 10 inches (25 cm).

Switch to smaller dpns and work garter rib in the round:

Round 1: * k2, p2 * repeat from * to * across rnd.

Round 2: Knit.

Repeat these 2 rounds for 8 inches (20 cm) or to desired sleeve length. BO all sts kw.

Finishing:

Weave in ends, sewing up the tiny opening under the armhole. Seam inner pocket edges to side of sweater on each side.

Block by soaking garment for 20-30 minutes in a no-rinse solution for handknits. Lay out sweater, according to measurements shown on the schematic, and allow to air dry.

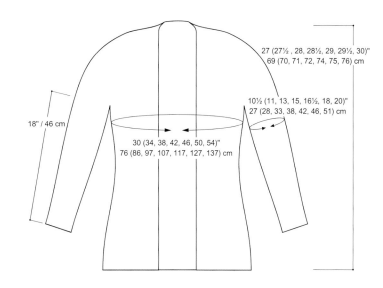

27 (27½ , 28, 28½, 29, 29½, 30)"
69 (70, 71, 72, 74, 75, 76) cm

10½ (11, 13, 15, 16½, 18, 20)"
27 (28, 33, 38, 42, 46, 51) cm

18" / 46 cm

30 (34, 38, 42, 46, 50, 54)"
76 (86, 97, 107, 117, 127, 137) cm

Lover's Lane first bridge, ca. 1890's. Cavendish, P.E.I. L.M. Montgomery Collection, Archival and Special Collections, University of Guelph Library.

"We are going to be the best of friends," said Gilbert, jubilantly. "We were born to be good friends, Anne. You've thwarted destiny long enough... Come, I'm going to walk home with you."

Gilbert's Scarf

Finished Measurements

Width: 6½ inches (16.5 cm). Length: 62 inches (158 cm).

Yarn

Brown Sheep Company Lanaloft Worsted; 100% Wool; 160 yards (146 meters) per 100 gram skein; color shown, Dark Ash; 2 skeins.

Needles

Size US 8 (5.0 mm) circular or straight needles

Change needle size if necessary to obtain the correct gauge.

Notions

Tapestry needle and blocking wires as preferred.

Gauge

18 sts 24 rows = 4" (10 cm) in stockinette stitch after blocking.

Because of the slip-stitch technique used in this pattern, it is likely that your scarf will roll up as you are knitting it. Never fear, this will be remedied by blocking the scarf carefully, as instructed in the pattern, when you have completed it.

Notes

The classic diagonal herringbone stitch on this scarf is created using slipped stitches. All slipped stitches are worked with the yarn in front, which is noted in the pattern as "wyif."

Difficulty Level:

Pattern

Cast on 30 sts.

Begin working in 12 row repeat back and forth as follows:

Row 1: Purl.

Row 2: * sl 3 wyif, k3 * repeat across row.

Row 3: Purl.

Row 4: K1, * sl 3 wyif, k3 * repeat from * to * ending k2 instead of k3.

Row 5: Purl.

Row 6: K2, * sl 3 wyif, k3 * repeat from * to * ending k1 instead of k3.

Row 7: Purl.

Row 8: * k3, sl 3 wyif * repeat from * to * across row.

Row 9: Purl.

Row 10: Sl 1 wyif, * k3, sl 3 wyif * repeat from * to * ending sl 2 instead of sl 3.

Row 11: Purl.

Row 12: sl 2 wyif, * k3, sl 3 wyif * repeat from * to * ending sl 1 instead of sl 3.

Repeat 12-row pattern until scarf reaches desired length.

Finishing:

Weave in ends.

Block by soaking scarf for 20-30 minutes in a no-rinse solution for handknits. Stretch scarf to desired dimensions and allow to air dry, using pins or blocking wires as preferred.

Lucy Maud Montgomery's old room in grandparents MacNeill's home, ca. 1880's. Cavendish, P.E.I.
L.M. Montgomery Collection, Archival and Special Collections, University of Guelph Library.

Archival photographs printed with permission, L. M. Montgomery Collection, Archival and Special Collections, University of Guelph Library.

L. M. Montgomery is a trademark of Heirs of L. M. Montgomery, Inc. Anne of Green Gables and other indicia of "Anne" are trademarks and Canadian Official Marks of the Anne of Green Gables Licensing Authority Inc. "L. M. Montgomery" and "L. M. Montgomery's signature and cat design" are trademarks of Heirs of L. M. Montgomery, Inc.

Deepest thanks to:

Kate Macdonald Butler and Heirs of L. M. Montgomery, Inc. for their interest in this book project. Pam O'Reilly and Kathryn Harvey at the University of Guelph Archival and Special Collections Department, for providing access to the archival photographs. Sally Keefe Cohen, Literary Consultant, for her clear and helpful communication. Peggy Jo Wells and the wonderful staff at Brown Sheep Company for offering their yarn for all of the patterns in this book. Christa Tippmann Photography, for capturing the spirit of this book through her lens. Hadley Austin, my tech editor, for her patience and attentiveness. Megan Helzer, my copy editor and test knitter, for her care and encouragement. Karen DeGeal, my test knitter and sample knitter, for her expertise. The City of Loveland Parks and Recreation Department, for maintaining such lovely parks and public spaces. Mrs. Johnson, the teacher at the Lone Tree Schoolhouse, for her support. Alan and Judy Johnson, for the use of their beautiful home.

Our models: Cathy Ballenski, Phil Ballenski, Susanna Ballenski, Laurel Johnson, Josh Lewis, Kristi Lichtfuss and Raceine Tippmann, for their eagerness to be a part of this project.

Our test knitters: Joyce Bensen, my mom, for everything; Dwala Canon, for her carefulness; Amelia Chapman, her willingness; Beth Elston, my sister, for her enthusiasm; Krista Elston, for stepping up at the last minute; Mari Liestman, for being inspiring; Erin McLaughlin, for her patience; Pam Miller, for being cheerful; Evangeline Snyder, for her encouragement; and Emily Straw, for her thoughtfulness.

My husband and book designer, Eric, and our three wonderful children, for their continued love and encouragement, and for the joy they bring to my life. God, for loving and guiding me.

Yarn Source: Brown Sheep Company 100662 CR 16 Mitchell, NE 69357 phone: 800.826.9136 web: brownsheep.com